THIS JOURNAL BELONGS TO:

www.ingramcontent.com/pod-product-compliance
Lightning Source LLC
Chambersburg PA
CBHW070233220526
45465CB00004B/1410